The Twelve Keys

of

Basil Valentine

also called

The Great Stone of the Ancient Sages

of

Basilius Valentinus,
the Benedictine

The Preface
of
Basilius Valentinus, the Benedictine

Concerning
The Great Stone of the
Ancient Sages.

When I had emptied to the dregs the cup of human suffering, I was led to consider the wretchedness of this world, and the fearful consequences of our first parents' disobedience. Then I saw that there was no hope of repentance for mankind, that they were getting worse day by day, and that for their impenitence God's everlasting punishment was hanging over them; and I made haste to withdraw myself from the evil world, to bid farewell to it, and to devote myself to the service of God.

When I had spent some years at the monastery, I found that after I had performed my work and my daily devotions I still had some time on my hands. This I did not wish to pass in idleness, lest my evil thoughts should lead me into new sins; and so I determined to use it for the study and investigation of those natural secrets by which God has shadowed out eternal things. So I read a great many books in our monastery written in olden times by philosophers who had pursued the same study, and was thereby stimulated to a more ardent desire of knowing that which they also knew. Though I did not make much progress at first, yet at last God granted my earnest prayer, and opened my eyes that I might see what others had seen before me.

In the convent there was a brother, who was afflicted with a severe disease of the kidneys, and to whom none of the many physicians he had consulted had been able to give even momentary relief. So he had committed himself to the hand of God, and despaired of all human aid.

As I loved him, I gathered all manner of herbs, extracted their salts, and distilled various medicines. But none of them seemed to do him the slightest good, and after six years I found that I had tried every possible vegetable substance, without any beneficial effect.

At last I determined to devote myself to the study of the powers and virtues which God has laid into metals and minerals and the more I searched the more I found. One discovery led to another, and, after God had permitted unto me many experiments, I understood clearly the nature and properties, and the secret potency, imparted by God to minerals and metals.

Among the mineral substances I found one which exhibited many colours, and proved to be of the greatest efficacy in art. The spiritual essence of this substance I extracted, and therewith restored our sick brother, in a few days, to perfect health. For the strength of this spirit was so great as to quicken the prostrate spirit of my diseased brother, who, from that day to the day of his death, remembered me in his hourly prayers. And his prayers, together with my own diligence, so prevailed with God, that there was revealed to me that great secret which God ever conceals from those who are wise in their own conceits.

Thus have I been wishing to reveal to you in this treatise, as far as may be lawful to me, the Stone of the Ancients, that you, too, might possess the knowledge of this highest of earthly treasures for your health and comfort in this valley of sorrow. I write about it, not for my own good, but for that of posterity, and though my words be few and simple, that which they import is of immeasurable magnitude. Ponder them well, that you also may find the Rock which is the foundation Stone of truth, the temporal blessing, and the eternal reward.

The Tract of Basilius Valentinus, the Benedictine, Concerning the Great Stone of the Ancient Sages.

In the preface, gentle Reader, and zealous Student of this Art, I promised to communicate to you a knowledge of our Corner Stone, or Rock, of the process by which it is prepared, and of the substance from which it was already derived by those ancient Sages, to whom the secret of our Art was first revealed by God for the health and happiness of earthly life.

Let me assure you that I fully intend to fulfil my promise, and to be as plain with you as the rules of our Art permit, not misleading you by sophistical deceptions, but opening up to you the spring of all blessings even unto the fountain head. I propose to set forth what I have to say in a few simple, straightforward words, for I am no adept in the art of multiplying words; nor do I think that exuberance of language tends to clearness; on the contrary, I am convinced that it is many words that darken council. Let me tell you, then, that although many are engaged in the search after this Stone, it is nevertheless found but by very few. For God never intended that it should become generally known. It is rather to be regarded as a gift which He reserves for those favoured few, who love the truth, and hate falsehood, who study our Art earnestly by day and by night, and whose hearts are set upon God with an unfeigned affection.

Hence, if you would prepare our great and ancient Stone, I testify unto you in all truth that you must give diligent heed to my teaching, and before all things implore the gracious blessing of the Creator of all things. You must also truly repent you of all your sins, confessing the same, and firmly resolve to lead a good and holy life. It is also necessary that you should determine to shew your gratitude to God for His unspeakable Gift, by succouring the poor and the distressed, and by opening your hand and your heart to the needy. Then God will bless your labour, and reward your search with success, and yourself with a seat in Heaven as the fruit of your faith.

Do not despise the truthful writings of those who possessed the Stone before us. For, after the enlightening grace of God, it is from them that I received my knowledge. Let your study of them be increased and repeated often, lest you lose the thread of insight, and the lamp of understanding be extinguished.

Give yourself wholly to study, and be not flighty or doubleminded. Let your mind be like a firm Rock, in which all the various sayings of the Sages are reduced to the unity of their common meaning. For a man who is easily influenced in different directions is not likely to find the right path.

As our most ancient Stone is not derived from combustible things, you should cease to seek it in substances which cannot stand the test of fire. For this reason it is absurd to suppose that we can make any use of vegetable substances, though the Stone, too, is endowed 'with a principle of growth.

If our Stone were a vegetable substance, it would, like other vegetables, be consumed by fire, leaving only a certain salt. Ancient writers have, indeed, described our Stone as the vegetable Stone. But that name was suggested to them by the fact that it grows and increases in size, like a plant.

Know also that animals only multiply after their kind, and within their own species. Hence our Stone can only be prepared out of its own seed, from which it was taken in the beginning; and hence also you will perceive that the soul of an animal must not be the subject of this investigation. Animals are a class by themselves; nor can anything ever be obtained from them that is not animal in its nature. But our Stone, as it has been bequeathed to me by the Ancients, is derived from two things, and one thing, in which is concealed a third thing. This is the purest truth, and a most faithful saying. For male and female have from of old been regarded as one body, not from any external or visible consideration, but on account of the ardour of that mutual love which naturally draws them together into one; and as the male and female seed jointly represent the principle of propagation, so also the sperm of the matter out of which our Stone is made can be sown and increased. There are in our substance two supplementary kinds of seed, from which our Stone may be prepared and multiplied.

If you are a true lover of our Art, you will carefully weigh and ponder these words, lest, with other sophisticators, you fall into the dangerous pit prepared by the common enemy of man. But whence are you to obtain this seed? This question you may most easily answer by asking yourself another question. What do you want to develop from this seed, and what use do you wish to make of it? There can be no doubt, then that it must be the root, or first substance, of metals, from which all metals derive their origin. It is, therefore, necessary that we should now proceed to speak of the generation of the metals.

In the beginning, when the Spirit of God moved upon the face of the waters, and as yet all was involved in darkness, Almighty and Eternal God, Whose beginning and wisdom are from everlasting, by His inscrutable counsel created heaven and earth, and all that in them is, both visible and invisible, out of nothing. How the act of creation was accomplished I will not attempt to explain. This is a matter which is set forth to us in Holy Scripture, and must be apprehended by faith.

To each creature God gave its own seed, wherewith to propagate its kind, that in this way there might always be an increase of men and animals, plants and metals. Man was not to be able to produce new seed: he was only permitted to educe new forms of life out of that which already existed. The creating of seed God reserved to Himself For if man could create seed he would be equal to the Creator.

Know that our seed is produced in the following way. A celestial influence descends from above, by the decree and ordinance of God, and mingles with the astral proper ties. When this union has taken place, the two bring forth a third namely, an earth-like substance, which is the principle of our seed, of its first source, so that it can shew an ancestry, and from which three the elements, such as water, air, and earth, take their origin. These elements work underground in the form of fire, and there produce what Hermes, and all who have preceded me, call the three first principles, viz., the internal soul, the impalpable spirit, and visible bodies, beyond which we can find no earlier beginning of our Magistery.

In the course of time these three unite, and are changed through the action of fire into a palpable substance, viz., quicksilver, sulphur, and salt. If these three substances be mixed, they are hardened and coagulated into a perfect body, which represents the seed chosen and appointed by the Creator. This is a most important and certain truth. If the metallic soul, the metallic spirit, and the metallic form of body be present, there will also be metallic quicksilver, metallic sulphur, and metallic salt, which together make up the perfect metallic body.

If you cannot perceive what you ought to understand herein, you should not devote yourself to the study of philosophy.

Moreover, I tell you in few words, that you cannot obtain a metallic body except by perfectly joining these three principles into one. Know, also, that all animals are, like man, composed of flesh and blood, and also possess a vitalizing spirit, but are destitute of the rational soul which the Creator gave to man alone. Therefore, when animals die, they perish for ever. But when man yields up his mortal life into the hands of his Creator, his soul does not die. It returns, and is united to the glorified body, in which, after the Resurrection, soul and spirit dwell together once more in eternal glory, never to be separated again throughout all eternity.

Hence the rational soul of man makes him an abiding creature, and, though his body may seem to die, yet we know that he will live for ever. For to him death is only a process of purification, by means of which he is freed from his sins, and translated to another and better place. But there is no resurrection for the brute beasts, because they have no rational soul, for which alone our Lord and Saviour shed His blood.

For though a body may be vitalized by a spirit, yet it need not, therefore, be fixed, unless, indeed, it possess a rational soul, that strong bond between body and spirit, which represents their union, and resists all efforts to separate them. Where there is no soul, there is no hope of redemption. Nothing can be perfect or lasting without a soul. This is a profound and most important truth, which I feel in conscience bound to make known to my readers. Now, the spirits of metals have this property of fixedness in a greater or less degree; they are more or less volatile in proportion to the mutual fitness of their bodies and souls. A metal that has the three conditions of fixedness is not affected by fire or overcome by any other outward agent. But there is only one metal that fulfils these conditions, namely, gold. Silver also contains fixed mercury, and is not so quickly volatilised as the imperfect metals, but stands the trial of fire, and yields no food to voracious Saturn.

Amatory Venus is clothed with abundant colour, and her whole body is one pure tincture, not unlike the red colour which is found in the most precious of metals. But though her spirit is of good quality, her body is leprous, and affords no permanent substratum to the fixed tincture. Hence the soul has to share the fate of the imperfect body, and when the body dies the soul has to leave it. For its dwelling has been destroyed by fire, and it is without a house wherein to abide.

Fixed salt has imparted to warlike Mars a hard, firm, and durable body, which is evidence of the generosity of his soul; nor can fire be said to have much power over it. And if its strength be united to the beauty of Venus, I do not say but that a precious and harmonious result may be obtained. For the phlegmatic or humid quality of the Moon may be heated with the ardent blood of Venus, and the blackness of Venus removed with the strong salt of Mars.

You need not look for our metallic seed among the elements. It need not be sought so far back. If you can only rectify the Mercury, Sulphur, and Salt (understand, those of the Sages) until the metallic spirit and body are inseparably joined together by means of the metallic soul, you thereby firmly rivet the chain of love, and prepare the palace for the coronation.

These things represent a liquid key, comparable to the celestial influence, and a dry water joined to the terrestrial substance: all which are one thing, derived from three, and two, and one. If you understand this, you have already attained our Magistery. Then you must join the husband and wife together that each may feed upon the other's flesh and blood, and that so they may propagate their species a thousandfold.

Though I would fain reveal this matter to you more plainly and openly, I am prohibited from doing so by the law of God, and by the fear of His wrath, and of eternal lest the gift of the Most High should be abused.

If, however, you do not understand the theoretical part of my work, perhaps the practical part will serve to enlighten you more fully. I will therefore proceed to shew how, by the help of God, I was enabled to prepare the Stone of the Ancients, and, for your further instruction, I will add twelve keys, in which I give a figurative account of our Art.

Take a quantity of the best and finest gold, and separate it into its component parts by those media which Nature vouchsafes to those who are lovers of Art, as an anatomist dissects the human body. Thus change your gold back into what it was before it became gold; and thou shalt find the seed, the beginning, the middle, and the end-that from which our gold and its female principle are derived, viz., the pure and subtle spirit, the spotless soul, and the astral salt and balsam. When these three are united, we may call them the mercurial liquid: a water which was examined by Mercury, found by him to be pure and spotless, and therefore espoused by him as his wife. Of the two was born an incombustible oil; for Mercury became so proud that he hardly knew himself. He put forth eagle feathers, and devoured the slippery tail, of the Dragon, and challenged Mars to battle.

Then Mars summoned his horsemen, and bade them enclose Mercury in prison under the ward of Vulcan, until he should be liberated by one of the female sex. When this became known, the other Planets assembled and held a deliberation on the question, what would be the best and wisest course to adopt. When they were met together, Saturn first came forward, and delivered himself as follows:

" I, Saturn, the greatest of the planets in the firmament, declare here before you all, that I am the meanest and most unprofitable of all that are here present, that my body is weak, corruptible, and of a swarthy hue, but that, nevertheless, it is I that try you all. For having nothing that is fixed about me, I carry away with me all that is of a kindred nature. My wretchedness is entirely caused by that fickle and inconstant Mercury, by his careless and neglectful conduct. Therefore, I pray you, let us be avenged on him, shut him up in prison, and keep him there till he dies and is decomposed, nay, until not a drop of his blood is to be seen."

Then yellow Jupiter stepped forward, bent his knees, inclined his sceptre, and with great authority bade them carry out the demand of Saturn. He added that he would punish everyone who did not aid the execution of this sentence.

Then Mars presented himself, with sword drawn -- a sword that shone with many colours, and gave out a beautiful and unwonted splendour. This sword he gave to the warder Vulcan, and bade him slay Mercury, and burn him, together with his bones, to ashes. This Vulcan consented to do.

While he was executing his office, there appeared a beautiful lady in a long, silver robe, intertissued with many waters, who was immediately recognised as the Moon, the wife of the Sun. She fell on her knees, and with outspread hands, and flowing tears, besought them to liberate her husband -- the Sun -- from the prison in which, through the crafty wiles of Mercury, he was being detained by the Planets. But Vulcan refused to listen to her request; nor was he softened by the moving prayers of Lady Venus, who appeared in a crimson robe, intertissued with threads of green, and charmed all by the beauty of her countenance and the fragrance of the flowers which she bore in her hand. She interceded with Vulcan, the Judge, in the Chaldee tongue, and reminded him that a woman was to effect the deliverance of the prisoner. But even to her pleading he turned a deaf ear.

While they were still speaking the heaven was opened, and there came forth a mighty animal, with many thousands of young ones, which drove the warder before it, and opening its mouth wide, swallowed Venus, its fair helper, at the same time exclaiming with a loud voice: " I am born of woman, woman has propagated my seed, and therewith filled the earth Her soul is devoted to mine, and therefore I must be nourished with her blood." When the animal had said these words with a loud voice, it hastened into a certain chamber, and shut the door behind it; whither its voracious brood followed, drinking of the aforesaid incombustible oil, which they digested with the greatest ease, and thereby became even more numerous than they had been before. This they continued to do until they filled the whole world.

Then the learned men of that country were gathered together, and strove to discover the true interpretation of all they had seen. But they were unable to agree until there came forward a man of venerable age, with snowy locks and silvery beard, and arrayed in a flowing purple robe On his head he wore a crown set with brilliant carbuncles. His loins were girded with the girdle of life. His feet were bare, and his words penetrated to the depth of the human soul. He mounted the tribune, and bade the assembly listen to him in silence, since he was sent from above to explain to them the significance of what they had seen.

When perfect silence prevailed, he delivered himself as follows:

"Awake, O man, and behold the light, lest the darkness deceive thee! The Gods revealed to me this matter in a profound sleep. Happy is the man who knows the great works of the Divine power. Blessed is he whose eyes are opened to behold light where before they saw darkness.

"Two Stars are given by the Gods to man to lead him to great wisdom. Gaze steadily upon them, follow their lights, and you will find in them the secret of knowledge.

"The bird Phoenix, from the south, plucks out the heart of the mighty beast from the east. Give the animal from the east wings, that it may be on an equality with the bird from the south. For the animal from the east must be deprived of its lion's skin, and lose its wings. Then it must plunge in the salt water of the vast ocean, and emerge thence in renovated beauty. Plunge thy volatile spirits in a deep spring whose waters never fail, that they may become like their mother, who is hidden therein, and born of three.

"Hungary is my native land, the sky and the stars are my habitation, the earth is my spouse. Though I must die and be buried, yet Vulcan causes me to be born anew. Therefore, Hungary is my native land, and my mother encloses the whole world."

When all that were present had received these his sayings, he thus continued:

"Cause that which is above to be below; that which is visible, to be invisible; and that which is palpable, to become impalpable. Again, let that which is below become that which is above; let the invisible become visible, and the impalpable, palpable. Here you see the perfection of our Art, without any defect, or diminution. But that in which death and life, destruction and resurrection dwell, is a round sphere, with which the goddess of fortune drives her chariot, and imparts the gift of wisdom to men of God. Its proper name here upon earth, and for the human understanding, is 'All-in-All.'

"Let him who would know what this 'All-in-All' is, give the earth great wings, and make it fly upward through the air to the heavenly regions. Then singe its wings with fierce heat, and make it fall into the Red Sea, and there be drowned. Then dry up the water with fire and air till the earth reappears, and you will have 'All-in-All.'

"If you cannot find it in this way, look around upon the things that are in the world. Then you will find the ' All-in-All,' which is the attracting force of all metals and minerals derived from salt and sulphur, and twice born of Mercury. More I may not say about ' All-in-All,' since all is comprehended in all.

"My friends, blessed are ye if, by listening to the words of the wise, ye can find this great Stone, which has power to cure leprous and imperfect metallic bodies and to regenerate them; to preserve men in health, and procure for them a long life -- as it has hitherto kept the vital fire burning within me so long that I am weary of life, and yearn to die.

"For His wisdom and mercy, and for the gracious Gift which He has bestowed upon me so long ago, I am bound to render God thanks, now and evermore. Amen."

When the old man had thus spoken, he vanished from their sight.

But all who had heard him went each man to his house, and meditated on his words by day and by night.

Here follow the Twelve Keys
of Basilius Valentinus, the Benedictine,
with which we may open the doors
of the knowledge of the Most Ancient Stone
and unseal the Most Secret Fountain of Health.

PRIMA CLAVIS.

FIRST KEY

Let my friend know that no impure or spotted things are useful for our purpose. For there is nothing in their leprous nature capable of advancing the interests of our Art There is much more likelihood of that which is in itself good being spoiled by that which is impure. Everything that is obtained from the mines has its value, unless, indeed, it is adulterated. Adulteration, however, spoils its goodness and its efficacy.

As the physician purges and cleanses the inward parts of the body, and removes all unhealthy matter by means of his medicines, so our metallic substances must be purified and refined of all foreign matter, in order to ensure the success of our task. Therefore, our Masters require a pure, immaculate body, that is untainted with any foreign admixture, which admixture is the leprosy of our metals.

Let the diadem of the King be of pure gold, and let the Queen that is united to him in wedlock be chaste and immaculate.

If you would operate by means of our bodies, take a fierce grey wolf, which, though on account of its name it be subject to the sway of warlike Mars, is by birth the offspring of ancient Saturn, and is found in the valleys and mountains of the world, where he roams about savage with hunger. Cast to him the body of the King, and when he has devoured it, burn him entirely to ashes in a great fire. By this process the King will be liberated; and when it has been performed thrice the Lion has overcome the wolf, and will find nothing more to devour in him. Thus our Body has been rendered fit for the first stage of our work.

Know that this is the only right and legitimate way of purifying our substance: for the Lion purifies himself with the blood of the wolf, and the tincture of its blood agrees most wonderfully with the tincture of the Lion, seeing that the two liquids are closely akin to each other. When the Lion's hunger is appeased, his spirit becomes more powerful than before, and his eyes glitter like the Sun. His internal essence is now of inestimable value for the removing of all defects, and the healing of all diseases. He is pursued by the ten lepers, who desire to drink his blood; and all that are tormented with any kind of sickness are refreshed with this blood.

For whoever drinks of this golden fountain, experiences a renovation of his whole nature, a vanishing of all unhealthy matter, a fresh supply of blood, a strengthening of the heart and of all the vitals, and a permanent bracing of every limb. For it opens all the pores, and through them bears away all that prevents the perfect health of the body, but allows all that is beneficial to remain therein unmolested.

But let my friend be scrupulously careful to preserve the fountain of life limpid and clear. If any strange water be mixed with it, it is spoiled, and becomes positively injurious. If it still retain any of the solvent which has been used for its dissolution, you must carefully purge it off. For no corrosive can be of the least use for the prevention of internal diseases.

When a tree is found to bear sour and unwholesome fruit, its branches must be cut off, and scions of better trees grafted upon it. The new branches thereupon become organically united to the trunk; but though nourished with its sap, they thence forward produce good and pleasant fruit.

The King travels through six regions in the heavenly firmament, and in the seventh he fixes his abode. There the royal palace is adorned with golden tapestry. If you understand my meaning, this Key will open the first lock, and push back the first bolt; but if you do not, no spectacles or natural eyesight will enable you to understand what follows. But Lucius Papirius has instructed me not to say any more about this Key.

II. CLAVIS.

SECOND KEY

In the houses of the great are found various kinds of drink, of which scarcely two are exactly like each other in odour, colour, or taste. For they are prepared in a great variety of different ways. Nevertheless they are all drunk, and each is designed for its own special use. When the Sun gives out his rays, and sheds them abroad upon the clouds, it is commonly said that he is attracting water, and if he do it frequently, and thereby cause rain, it is called a fruitful year.

If it be intended to build a palace, the services of many different craftsmen must be employed, and a great variety of materials is required. Otherwise the palace would not be worthy the name. It is useless to use wood where stone is necessary.

The daily ebb and flow of the sea, which are caused by the sympathetic influence of heavenly bodies, impart great wealth and blessing to the earth. For whenever the water comes rolling back, it brings a blessing with it.

A bride, when she is to be brought forth to be married, is gloriously adorned in a great variety of precious garments, which, by enhancing her beauty, render her pleasant in the eyes of the bridegroom. But the rites of the bridal night she performs without any clothing but that which she was arrayed withal at the moment of her birth.

In the same way our bridal pair, Apollo and Diana, are arrayed in splendid attire, and their heads and bodies are washed with various kinds of water, some strong, some weak, but not one of them exactly like another, and each designed for its own special purpose. Know that when the moisture of the earth ascends in the form of a vapour, it is condensed in the upper regions, and precipitated to the earth by its own weight. Thus the earth regains the moisture of which it had been deprived, and receives strength to put forth buds and herbs. In the same way you must repeatedly distil the water which you have extracted from the earth, and then again restore it to your earth, as the water in the Strait of Euripus frequently leaves the shore, and then covers it again until it arrives at a certain limit.

When thus the palace has been constructed by the hands of many craftsmen, and the sea of glass has absolved its course, and filled the palace with good things, it is ready for the King to enter, and take his seat upon the throne. But you should notice that the King and his spouse must be quite naked when they are joined together. They must be stripped of all their glorious apparel, and must lie down together in the same state of nakedness in which they were born, that their seed may not be spoiled by being mixed with any foreign matter.

Let me tell you, in conclusion, that the bath in which the bridegroom is placed, must consist of two hostile kinds of matter, that purge and rectify each other by means of a continued struggle. For it is not good for the Eagle to build her nest on the summit of the Alps, because her young ones are thus in great danger of being frozen to death by the intense cold that prevails there.

But if you add to the Eagle the icy Dragon that has long had its habitation upon the rocks, and has crawled forth from the caverns of the earth, and place both over the fire, it will elicit from the icy Dragon a fiery spirit, which, by means of its great heat, will consume the wings of the Eagle, and prepare a perspiring bath of so extraordinary a degree of heat that the snow will melt upon the summit of the mountains, and become a water, with which the invigorating mineral bath may be prepared, and fortune, health, life, and strength restored to the King.

III. CLAVIS

THIRD KEY

By means of water fire may be extinguished, and utterly quenched. If much water be poured upon a little fire, the fire is overcome, and compelled to yield up the victory to the water. In the same way our fiery sulphur must be overcome by means of our prepared water. But, after the water has vanished, the fiery life of our sulphurous vapour must triumph, and again obtain the victory. But no such triumph can take place unless the King imparts great strength and potency to his water and tinges it with his own colour, that thereby he may be consumed and become invisible, and then again recover his visible form, with a diminution of his simple essence, and a development of his perfection.

A painter can set yellow upon white, and red or crimson upon yellow; for, though all these colours are present, yet the latter prevails on account of its greater intensity. When you have accomplished the same thing in our Art, you have before your eyes the light of wisdom, which shines in the darkness, although it does not burn. For our sulphur does not burn, but nevertheless its brilliancy is seen far and near. Nor does it colour anything until it has been prepared, and dyed with its own colour, which it then imparts to all weak and imperfect metals. This sulphur, however, cannot impart this colour until it have first by persevering labour been prevailed upon to abjure its original colour. For the weaker does not overcome the stronger, but has to yield the victory to it. The gist of the whole matter lies in the fact that the small and weak cannot aid that which is itself small and weak, and a combustible substance cannot shield another substance from combustion. That which is to protect another substance against combustion must itself be safe from danger. The latter must be stronger than the former, that is to say, it must itself be essentially incombustible. He, then, who would prepare the incombustible sulphur of the Sages, must look for our sulphur in a substance in which it is incombustible -- which can only be after its body has been absorbed by the salt sea, and again rejected by it. Then it must be so exalted as to shine more brightly than all the stars of heaven, and in its essence it must have an abundance of blood, like the Pelican, which wounds its own breast, and, without any diminution of its strength, nourishes and rears up many young ones with its blood. This Tincture is the Rose of our Masters, of purple hue, called also the red blood of the Dragon, or the purple cloak many times folded with which the Queen of Salvation is covered, and by which all metals are regenerated in colour.

Carefully preserve this splendid mantle, together with the astral salt which is joined to this sulphur, and screens it from harm. Add to it a sufficient quantity of the volatility of the bird; then the Cock will swallow the Fox, and, having been drowned in the water, and quickened by the fire, will in its turn be swallowed by the Fox.

FOURTH KEY

All flesh that is derived from the earth, must be decomposed and again reduced to earth; then the earthy salt produces a new generation by celestial resuscitation. For where there was not first earth, there can be no resurrection in our Magistery. For in earth is the balm of Nature, and the salt of the Sages.

At the end of the world, the world shall be judged by fire, and all those things that God has made of nothing shall by fire be reduced to ashes, from which ashes the Phoenix is to produce her young. For in the ashes slumbers a true and genuine tartaric substance, which, being dissolved, will enable us to open the strongest bolt of the royal chamber.

After the conflagration, there shall be formed a new heaven and a new earth, and the new man will be more noble in his glorified state than he was before.

When the sand and ashes have been well matured and ripened with fire, the glass-blower makes out of it glass, which remains hard and firm in the fire, and in colour resembles a crystal stone. To the uninitiated this is a great mystery, but not to the master whom long experience has familiarized with the process.

Out of stones the master also prepares lime by burning which is very useful for our work- But before they are prepared with fire, they are mere stones. The stone must be matured and rendered fervent with fire, and then it becomes so potent that few things are to be compared to the fiery spirit of lime.

By burning anything to ashes you may gain its salt. If in this dissolution the sulphur and mercury be kept apart, and restored to its salt, you may once more obtain that form which was destroyed by the process of combustion. This assertion the wise of this world denounce as the greatest folly, and count as a rebellion, saying that such a transformation would amount to a new creation, and that God has denied such creative power to sinful man. But the folly is all on their side. For they do not understand that our Artist does not claim to create anything, but only to evolve new things from the seed made ready to his hand by the Creator.

If you do not possess the ashes, you will be unable to obtain our salt; and without our salt you will not be able to impart to our substance a bodily form; for the coagulation of all things is produced by salt alone.

As salt is the great preserving principle that protects all things from decay, so the Salt of our Magistery preserves metal from decomposition and utter annihilation. If their Balm were to perish, and the Spirit to leave the body, the body would be quite dead, and no longer available for any good purpose. The metallic spirit would have departed, and would have left its habitation empty, bare, and lifeless.

Observe also, thou who art a lover of this Art, that the salt that is gained from ashes has great potency, and possesses many concealed virtues. Nevertheless, the salt is unprofitable, until its inward substance has been extracted. For the spirit alone gives strength and life. The body by itself profits nothing. If you know how to find this spirit, you have the Salt of the Sages, and the incombustible oil, concerning which many things have been written before my time.

Although many philosophers
Have sought for me with eagerness,
Yet very few succeed at length
In finding out my secret virtue.

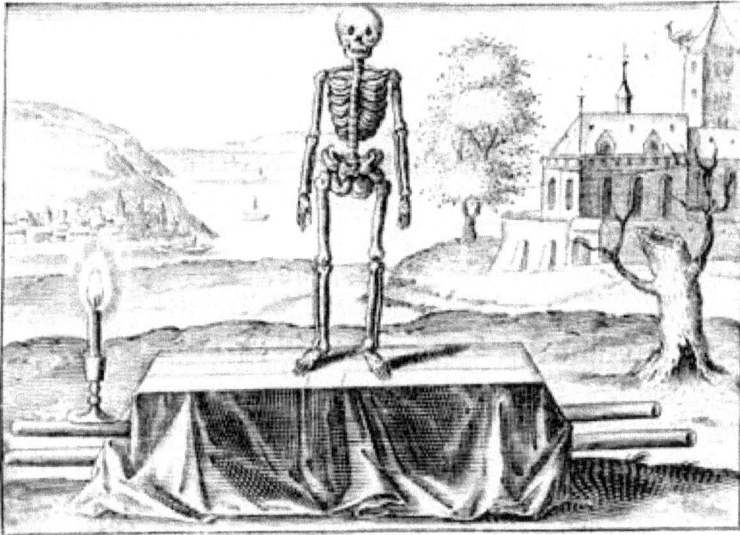

FIFTH KEY

The quickening power of the earth produces all things that grow forth from it, and he who says that the earth has no life makes a statement which is flatly contradicted by the most ordinary facts. For what is dead cannot produce life and growth, seeing that it is devoid of the quickening spirit. This spirit is the life and soul that dwell in the earth, and are nourished by heavenly and sidereal influences. For all herbs, trees, and roots, and all metals and minerals, receive their growth and nutriment from the spirit of the earth, which is the spirit of life. This spirit is itself fed by the stars, and is thereby rendered capable of imparting nutriment to all things that grow, and of nursing them as a mother does her child while it is yet in the womb. The minerals are hidden in the womb of the earth, and nourished by her with the spirit which she receives from above.

Thus the power of growth that I speak of is imparted not by the earth, but by the life-giving spirit that is in it. If the earth were deserted by this spirit, it would be dead, and no longer able to afford nourishment to anything. For its sulphur or richness would lack the quickening spirit without which there can be neither life nor growth.

Two contrary spirits can scarcely dwell together, nor do they easily combine. For when a thunderbolt blazes amidst a tempest of rain, the two spirits, out of which it is formed, fly from one another with a great shock and noise, and circle in the air, so that no one can know or say whither they go, unless the same has been ascertained by experience as to the mode in which these spirits manifest.

Know then, gentle Reader, that life is the only true spirit, and that that which the ignorant herd look upon as dead may be brought back to permanent, visible, and spiritual life, if but the spirit be restored to the body -- the spirit which is supported by heavenly nutriment, and derived from heavenly, elementary, and earthly substances, which are also called formless matter. Moreover, as iron has its magnet which draws it with the invisible bonds of love, so our gold has its magnet, viz., the first Matter of the great Stone. If you understand these my words, you are richer and more blessed than the whole world.

Let me conclude this chapter with one more remark. When a man looks into a mirror, he sees therein reflected an image of himself. If, however, he try to touch it, he will find that it is not palpable, and that he has laid his hand upon the mirror only. In the same way, the spirit which must be evolved from this Matter is visible, but not palpable. This spirit is the root of the life of our bodies, and the Mercury of the Philosophers, from which is prepared the liquid water of our Art - the water which must once more receive a material form, and be rectified by means of certain purifying agents into the most perfect Medicine. For we begin with a firm and palpable body, which subsequently becomes a volatile spirit, and a golden water, without any conversion, from which our Sages derive their principle of life. Ultimately we obtain the indestructible medicine of human and metallic bodies, which is fitter to be known to angels than to men, except such as seek it at God's hands in heartfelt prayer, and give genuine proofs of their gratitude by service rendered to Him, and to their needy neighbour.

Hereunto I may add, in conclusion, that one work is developed from another. First, our Matter should be carefully purified, then dissolved, destroyed, decomposed, and reduced to dust and ashes. Thereupon prepare from it a volatile spirit, which is white as snow, and another volatile spirit, which is red as blood. These two spirits contain a third, and are yet but one spirit. Now these are the three spirits which preserve and multiply life. Therefore unite them, give them the meat and drink that Nature requires, and keep them in a warm chamber until the perfect birth takes place. Then you will see and experience the virtue of the gift bestowed upon you by God and Nature. Know, also, that hitherto my lips have not revealed this secret to any one, and that God has endowed natural substances with greater powers than most men are ready to believe. Upon my mouth God has set a seal, that there might be scope for others after me to write about the wonderful things of Nature, which by the foolish are looked upon as unnatural. For they do not understand that all things are ultimately traceable to supernatural causes, but nevertheless are, in this present state of the world, subject to natural conditions.

VI. CLAVIS.

SIXTH KEY

The male without the female is looked upon as only half a body, nor can the female without the male be regarded as more complete For neither can bring forth fruit so long as it remains alone. But if the two be conjugally united, there is a perfect body, and their seed is placed in a condition in which it can yield increase.

If too much seed be cast into the field, the plants impede each other's growth, and there can be no ripe fruit. But if, on the other hand, too little be sown, weeds spring up and choke it.

If a merchant would keep a clear conscience, let him give just measure to his neighbour. If his measure and weight be not short, he will receive praise from the poor.

In too much water you may easily be drowned; too little water, on the other hand, soon evaporates in the heat of the sun.

If, then, you would attain the longed-for goal, observe just measure in mixing the liquid substance of the Sages, lest that which is too much overpower that which is too little, and the generation be hindered. For too much rain spoils the fruit, and too much drought stunts its growth. Therefore, when Neptune has prepared his bath, measure out carefully the exact quantity of permanent water needed, and let there be neither too little nor too much.

The twofold fiery male must be fed with a snowy swan, and then they must mutually slay each other and restore each other to life; and the air of the imprisoned fiery male will occupy three of the four quarters of the world, and make up three parts of the imprisoned fiery male, that the death-song of the swans may be distinctly heard; then the swan roasted will become food for the King, and the fiery King will be seized with great love towards the Queen, and will take his fill of delight in embracing her, until they both vanish and coalesce into one body.

It is commonly said that two can overpower one, especially if they have sufficient room for putting forth their strength. Know also that there must come a twofold wind, and a single wind, and that they must furiously blow from the east and from the south. lf, when they cease to rage, the air has become water, you may be confident that the spiritual will also be transmuted into a bodily form, and that our number shall prevail through the four seasons in the fourth part of the sky (after the seven planets have exercised power), and that its course will be perfected by the test of fire in the lowest chamber of our palace, when the two shall overpower and consume the third.

For this part of our Magistery skill is needed, in order to divide and compound the substances aright, so that the art may result in riches, and the balance may not be falsified by unequal weights. The sky we speak of is the sky of our Art, and there must be justly proportioned parts of our air and earth, our true water and our palpable fire.

VII. CLAVIS.

SEVENTH KEY

Natural heat preserves the life of man. If his body lose its natural heat his life has come to an end.

A moderate degree of natural heat protects against the cold; an excess of it destroys life. It is not necessary that the substance of the Sun should touch the earth. The Sun can heat the earth by shedding thereon its rays, which are intensified by reflection. This intermediate agency is quite sufficient to do the work of the Sun, and to mature everything by coction. The rays of the Sun are tempered with the air by passing through it so as to operate by the medium of the air, as the air operates through the medium of the fire.

Earth without water can produce nothing, nor can water quicken anything into growth without earth; and as earth and water are mutually indispensable in the production of fruit, so fire cannot operate without air, or air without fire. For fire has no life without air; and without fire air possesses neither heat nor dryness.

When its fruit is about to be matured, the vine stands in greater need of the Sun's warmth than in the spring; and if the Sun shine brightly in the autumn, the grapes will be better than if they had not felt his autumnal warmth.

In the winter the multitude suppose everything to be dead, because the earth is bound in the chains of frost, so that nothing is allowed to sprout forth. But as soon as the spring comes, and the cold is vanquished by the power of the Sun, everything is restored to life, the trees and herbs put forth buds, leaves, and blossoms, the hibernating animals creep forth from their hiding places, the plants give out a sweet fragrance, and are adorned with a great variety of many coloured flowers; and the summer carries on the work of the spring, by changing its flowers into fruit.

Thus, year by year, the operations of the universe are performed, until at length it shall be destroyed by its Creator, and all the dwellers upon earth shall be restored by resurrection to a glorified life. Then the operations of earthly nature shall cease, and the heavenly and eternal dispensation shall take its place.

When the Sun in the winter pursues his course far away from us, he cannot melt the deep snow. But in the summer he approaches nearer to us, the quality of the air becomes more fiery, and the snow melts and is transmuted by warmth into water. For that which is weak is always compelled to yield to that which is strong.

The same moderate course must be adopted in the fiery regimen of our Magistery. For it is all important that the liquid should not be dried up too quickly, and that the earth of the Sages should not be melted and dissolved too soon, otherwise your fishes would be changed into scorpions. If you would perform our task rightly, take the spiritual water, in which the spirit was from the beginning, and preserve it in a closely shut chamber. For the heavenly city is about to be besieged by earthly foes. You must, therefore, strongly fortify it with three impassable and well-guarded walls, and let the one entrance be well protected. Then light the lamp of wisdom and seek with it the gross thing that was lost, shewing only such light as is needed. For you must know that the worms and reptiles dwell in the cold and humid earth, while man has his proper habitation upon the face of the earth; the bodies of angels, on the other hand, not being alloyed with sin or impurity, are injured by no extreme either of heat or cold. When man shall have been glorified, his body will become like the angelic body in this respect. If we carefully cultivate the life of our souls, we shall be sons and heirs of God, and shall be able to do that which now seems impossible. But this can be effected only by the drying up of all water, and the purging of heaven and earth and all men with fire

VIII. CLAVIS.

EIGHTH KEY

Neither human nor animal bodies can be multiplied or propagated without decomposition; the grain and all vegetable seed, when cast into the ground, must decay before it can spring up again; moreover, putrefaction imparts life to many worms and other animalculae. The process of augmentation and quickening is mostly performed in [the] earth, while it is caused by spiritual seed through the other elements.

The farmer's wife knows that she cannot hope to obtain chickens except through the decomposition of the egg. If bread is placed in honeys and suffered to decay, ants are generated; worms are bred in the putrefying bodies of men, horses, and other animals; maggots are also developed by the decay of nuts, apples, and pears.

The same thing may be observed in regard to vegetable life. Nettles and other weeds spring up where no such seed has ever been sown. This occurs only by putrefaction. The reason is that the soil in such places is so disposed, and, as it were, impregnated, that it produces these fruits, which is a result of the properties of sidereal influence; consequently the seed is spiritually produced in the earth, and putrefies in the earth, and by the operation of the elements generates corporeal matter according to the species of Nature. Thus the stars and the elements may generate new spiritual, and, ultimately, new vegetable seed, by means of putrefaction. But man cannot create new seed; for it is not in his power to order the operation of the elements and the essential influences of the stars. By natural conditions, however, new plants are generated simply through putrefaction. This fact is not noticed by the farmer, simply because it is a thing that he has always been used to, and for which he is unable to find an explanation. But you who should know more than the vulgar herd, must search into the causes of things, and endeavor to understand how the process of generation and resuscitation is accomplished by means of decomposition, and how all life is produced out of decay.

Each element is in its turn decomposed and regenerated by that which is contained in it. For you should know that every element contains the three others. In air, for instance, there is fire, water, and earth. This assertion may appear incredible, but it is nevertheless true. In like manner, fire includes air, water, and earth, since otherwise it could generate nothing. Water contains fire, air, and earth; for if it did not, there could be no growth. At the same time, each element is distinct, though each contains the others. All this is: found by distillation in the separation of the elements.

In order to rationally prove this to you, who are investigating the separation of Nature. and purpose to understand the division of the elements, lest you should think my words inventions, and not true, I tell you that if you distil earth, you will find that, first of all, there is an escape of air, which, in its turn, always contains fire, as they are both of a spiritual essence, and exercise an irresistible mutual attraction. In the next place, there issues water from the earth, and the earth, in which is the precious salt, remains by itself at the bottom of the vessel.

When water is distilled, air and fire issue from it, and the water and material earth remain at the bottom. Again, when the invisible part of elementary fire is extracted, you get water and earth by themselves. Nor can any of the three other elements exist without air. It is air that gives to earth its power of production, to fire its power of burning, to water its power of generating fruit. Again, air can consume nothing, nor dry up any moisture, without that natural heat which must be imparted to it by fire. For everything that is hot and dry contains fire. From these considerations we conclude that no element can exist without the others, and that in the generation of all things there is a mingling of the four elements. He who states the contrary in no wise understands the secrets of Nature, nor has he investigated the properties of the elements. For if anything is to be generated by putrefaction, the process must be as follows: The earth is first decomposed by the moisture which it contains; for without moisture, or water, there can be no true decay; thereupon the decomposed substance is kindled and quickened by the natural heat of fire: for without natural heat no generation can take place. Again, if that which has received the spark of life, is to be stirred up to motion and growth, it must be acted upon by air. For without air, the quickened substance would be choked and stifled in the germ. Hence it manifestly appears that no one element can work effectually without the aid of the others, and that all must contribute towards the generation of anything. Thus their quickening cooperation takes the form of putrefaction, without which there can be neither generation, life, nor growth. That there can be no perfect generation or resuscitation without the co-operation of the four elements, you may see from the fact that when Adam had been formed by the Creator out of earth, there was no life in him, until God breathed into him a living spirit. Then the earth was quickened into motion. In the earth was the salt that is, the Body; the air that was breathed into it was mercury or the Spirit, and this air imparted to him a genuine and temperate heat, which was sulphur, or fire. Then Adam moved and by his power of motion, shewed that there had been infused into him a life-giving spirit. For as there is no fire without air so neither is there any air without fire. Water was incorporated with the earth Thus living man is an harmonious mixture of the four elements; and Adam was generated out of earth, water, air, and fire, out of soul, spirit, and body, out of mercury, sulphur, and salt.

In the same way, Eve, our common mother, was created; for her body was built up and formed out of Adam's body - a fact which I wish you particularly to notice.

To return again to putrefaction, O seeker of the Magistery and devotee of philosophy, know that, in like manner, no metallic seed can develop, or multiply, unless the said seed, by itself alone, and without the introduction of any foreign substance, be reduced to a perfect putrefaction.

The putrefaction of metallic seed must, like that of animal and vegetable seed, take place through the co-operation of the four elements. I have already explained that the elements themselves are not the seed. But it ought by this time to be clear to you that the metallic seed which was produced by the combined operation of heavenly, sidereal, and elementary essences, and reduced into bodily form, must, in due course, be corrupted and putrefied by means of the elements.

Observe that this seed contains a living volatile spirit. For when it is distilled, there issues from it first a spirit, and then that which is less volatile. But when by continued gentle heat, it is reduced to an acid, the spirit is not so volatile as it was before. For in the distillation of the acid the water issues first, and then the spirit. And though the substance remains the same, its properties have become very different. It is no longer wine, but has been transmuted by the putrefaction of gentle heat into an acid. That which is extracted with wine or its spirit, has widely different properties and powers from that which is extracted with an acid. For if the crystal of antimony be extracted with wine or the spirit of wine, it causes vomiting and diarrhoea, because it is a poison, and its poisonous quality is not destroyed by the wine. But if it be extracted with a good distilled acid, it furnishes a beautiful extract of a rich colour. If the acid be removed by means of the St. Mary's Bath, and the residuum of yellow powder washed away, you obtain a sweet powder which causes no diarrhoea, but is justly regarded as a marvellously beneficial medicine.

This excellent powder is dissolved in a moist place into a liquid which is profitably employed as a painless agent in surgery.

Let me sum up in few words what I have to say. The substance is of heavenly birth, its life is preserved by the stars, and nourished by the four elements; then it must perish, and be putrefied; again, by the influence of the stars, which works through the elements, it is restored to life, and becomes once more a heavenly thing that has its habitation in the highest region of the firmament. Then you will find that the heavenly has assumed an earthly body, and that the earthly body has been reduced to a heavenly substance.

IX. CLAVIS,

NINTH KEY

Saturn, who is called the greatest of the planets, is the least useful in our Magistery. Nevertheless, it is the chief Key of the whole Art, howbeit set in the lowest and meanest place. Although by its swift flight it has risen to the loftiest height, far above all other luminaries, its feathers must be clipped, and itself brought down to the lowest place, from whence it may once more be raised by putrefaction, and the quickening caused by putrefaction, by which the black is changed to white, and the white to red, until the glorious colour of the triumphant King has been attained.

Therefore, I say that though Saturn may seem the vilest thing in the world, yet it has such power and effficacy that if its precious essence, which is excessively cold, be reduced to a metallic body by being deprived of its volatility, it becomes as corporeal as, but far more fixed than, Saturn itself. This transmutation is begun, continued, and completed with Mercury, sulphur, and salt. This will seem unintelligible to many, and it certainly does make an extraordinary demand upon the mental faculties; but that must be so because the substance is within the reach of everyone, and there is no other way of keeping up the divinely ordained difference between rich and poor.

In the preparation of Saturn there appears a great variety of different colours; and you must expect to observe successively black, grey, white, yellow, red, and all the different intermediate shades. In the same way, the Matter of all the Sages passes through the several varieties of colour, and may be said to change its appearance as often as a new gate of entrance is opened to the fire.

The King shares his royal dignity with noble Venus, and appears in splendid state, surrounded by all the dignitaries of his court. Before him is borne a beautiful crimson banner, in which there is an embroidered representation of Charity in green garments. Saturn is the prefect of the royal household, and in front of him Astronomy bears a black standard, with a representation of Faith in yellow and red garments.

Jupiter is the Grand Marshal, and is preceded by a banner of grey colour, borne by Rhetoric, and adorned with a variegated representation of Hope.

Mars is at the head of military affairs, and executes his office with a certain fiery ardour. Geometry carries before him a crimson banner, on which you may behold Courage in a crimson cloak. Mercury holds the office of Chancellor; Arithmetic is his standard bearer, and his standard is of many colours; on it may be observed the figure of Temperance in a many coloured robe.

The Sun is Vice-Regent, and is preceded by Grammar, bearing a yellow banner, on which Justice is represented in a golden robe Though Venus seems to cast him into the shade by the gorgeous magnificence of her appearance, he really possesses more power in the kingdom than she.

Before the Moon, Dialectic bears a shining silver banner, with the figure of Prudence wrought into it in sky-blue, and because the husband of the Moon is dead, he has transferred to her his task of resisting the domination of Queen Venus. For among all these there is enmity, and they are all striving to supplant each other. Indeed, the tendency of events is to give the highest place to the most excellent and the most deserving. For the present state of things is passing away, and a new world is about to be created, and one Planet is devouring another spiritually, until only the strongest survive.

Let me tell you allegorically that you must put into the heavenly Balance the Ram, Bull, Cancer, Scorpion, and Goat. In the other scale of the Balance you must place the Twins, the Archer, the Water-bearer, and the Virgin. Then let the Lion jump into the Virgin's lap, which will cause the other scale to kick the beam. Thereupon, let the signs of the Zodiac enter into opposition to the Pleiads, and when all the colours of the world have shewn themselves, let there be a conjunction and union between the greatest and the smallest, and the smallest and the greatest.

If the whole world's nature
Were seen in one figure,
And nothing could be evolved by Art,
Nothing wonderful would be found in the Universe,
And Nature would have nothing to tell us.
For which let us laud and praise God.

X. CLAVIS.

NATVS SVM EX HERMOGENE.

TENTH KEY

In our Stone, as composed by me and by those who have long preceded me, are contained all elements, all mineral and metallic forms, and all the qualities and properties of the whole world. In it we find most powerful natural heat, by which the icy body of Saturn is gently transmuted into the best gold. It contains also a high degree of cold, which tempers the fervent heat of Venus, and coagulates the mercury, which is thereby also changed into the finest gold. All these properties slumber in the substance of our Stone, and are developed, perfected, and matured by the gentle coction of natural fire, until they have attained their highest perfection. If the fruit of a tree be plucked before it is ripe, it is unfit for use; and if the potter fail to harden his vessels in the fire, they cannot be employed for any good purpose.

In the same way you must exercise considerable patience in preparing our Elixir, if it is to become all that you wish it to become. No fruit can grow from a flower that has been plucked before the time. He who is in too great a hurry, can bring nothing to perfection, but is almost sure to spoil that which he has in hand. Remember, then, that if our Stone be not sufficiently matured, it will not be able to bring anything to maturity.

The substance is dissolved in a bath, and its parts reunited by putrefaction. In ashes it blossoms. In the form of sand all its excessive moisture is dried up. Maturity and fixity are obtained by living fire. The work does not actually take place in the Bath of St. Mary, in horse- dung, in ashes, or in sand, but the grades and regimen of the fire proceed after the degrees which are represented by these The Stone is prepared in an empty furnace, with a threefold line of circumvallation, in a tightly closed chamber. It is subjected to continued coction, till all moisture and clouds are driven off, and the King attains to indestructible fixedness, and is no longer liable to any danger or injury, because he has become unconquerable. Let me express my meaning in a somewhat different manner. When you have dissolved your earth with your water, dry up the water with its own inward fire. Then the air will breathe new life into the body, and you will have that which can only be regarded as that Great Stone which in a spiritual manner pervades human and metallic bodies, and is the universal and immaculate Medicine, since it drives out that which is bad, and preserves that which is good, and is the unfailing corrective of all imperfect or diseased substances. This Tincture Is of a colour intermediate between red and purple, with something of a granite hue, and its specific weight is very considerable.

Whoever gains possession of this Stone, should let his whole life he an expression of his gratitude towards God in practical kindness towards his suffering brethren, that after obtaining God's greatest earthly gift, he may hereafter inherit eternal life. Praise be unto God everlastingly for this His inestimable gift.

XI. CLAVIS.

ELEVENTH KEY

The eleventh Key to the Knowledge of the augmentation of our Stone, I will put before you in the form of a parable.

There lived in the East a gilded knight, named Orpheus, who was possessed of immense wealth, and had everything that heart can wish. He had taken to wife his own sister, Euridice, who did not, however, bear him any children. This he regarded as the punishment of his sin in having wedded his own sister, and was instant in prayer to God both by day and by night, that the curse might be taken from him.

One night, when he was buried in a deep sleep, there came to him a certain winged messenger, named Phoebus, who touched his feet, which were very hot, and said: " Thou noble knight, since thou hast wandered through many cities and kingdoms, and suffered many things at sea, in battle, and in the lists, the heavenly Father has bidden me make known to thee the following means of obtaining thy prayer: Take blood from thy right side, and from the left side of thy spouse. For this blood is the heart's blood of your parents, and though it may seem to be of two kinds, yet, in reality, it is only one. Mix the two kinds of blood, and keep the mixture tightly enclosed in the globe of the seven wise Masters There that which is generated will be nourished with its own flesh and blood, and will complete its course of development when the Moon has changed for the eighth time If thou repeat this process again and again, thou shalt see children's children, and the offspring of thy body shall fill the world."

When Phoebus had thus spoken, he winged his flight heavenward. In the morning the knight arose and did the bidding of the celestial messenger, and God gave to him and to his wife many children, who inherited their father's glory, wealth, and knightly honours from generation to generation.

If you are wise, my son, you will find the interpretation of my parable. If you do not understand it, ascribe the blame not to me, but to your own ignorance. I may not express myself more explicitly; indeed, I have revealed the matter in a more plain and straightforward manner than any of my predecessors. 1 have concealed nothing; and if you will but remove the veil of ignorance from your eyes, you will behold that which many have sought and few found.

XII. CLAVIS

TWELFTH KEY

If an athlete know not the use of his sword, he might as well be without it; and if another warrior that is skilled in the use of that weapon come against him, the first is like to fare badly. For he that has knowledge and experience on his side, must carry off the victory.

In the same way, he that possesses this tincture, by the grace of Almighty God, and is unacquainted with its uses, might as well not have it at all. Therefore this twelfth and last Key must serve to open up to you the uses of this Stone. In dealing with this part of the Subject I will drop my parabolic and figurative style, and plainly set forth all that is to be known. When the Medicine and Stone of all the Sages has been perfectly prepared out of the true virgin's milk, take one part of it to three parts of the best gold purged and refined with antimony, the gold being previously beaten into plates of the greatest possible thinness. Put the whole into a smelting pot and subject it to the action of a gentle fire for twelve hours, then let it be melted for three days and three nights more.

For without the ferment of gold no one can compose the Stone or develop the tinging virtue. For the same is very subtle and penetrating if it be fermented and joined with a ferment like unto itself: then the prepared tincture has the power of entering into other bodies, and operating therein. Take then one part of the prepared ferment for the tinging of a thousand parts of molten metal, and then you will learn in all faith and truth that it shall be changed into the only good and fixed gold. For one body takes possession of the other; even if it be unlike to it, nevertheless, through the strength and potency added to it, it is compelled to be assimilated to the same, since like derives origin from like.

Whoever uses this as a medium shall find whither the vestibules of the palace lead, and there is nothing comparable to the subtlety thereof. He shall possess all in all, performing all things whatsoever which are possible under the sun.

O principle of the prime principle, consider the end! O end of the final end, consider the beginning! And be this medium commended unto your faithful care, wherein also God the Father, Son, and Holy Ghost, shall give unto you whatsoever you need both in soul and body.

Concerning the First Matter
of the Philosophical Stone

Seek for that Stone which has no fleshly nature, but out of which a volatile fire is extracted, whence also this stone is made, being composed of white and red. It is a stone, and no stone; therein Nature alone operates. A fountain flows from it. The fixed part submerges its father, absorbing it, body and life, until the soul is returned to it. And the volatile mother like to him, is produced in her own kingdom; and he by his virtue and power receives greater strength. The volatile mother when prepared surpasses the sun in summer. Thus the father by means of Vulcan was produced from the spirit. Body, soul, and spirit exist in both, whence the whole matter proceeds. It proceeds from one, and is one matter. Bind together the fixed and the volatile; they are two, and three, and yet one only. If you do not understand you will attain nothing. Adam was in a bath -- wherein Venus found her like, which bath the aged Dragon had prepared when his strength was deserting him. There is nothing, says the Philosopher, save a double mercury; I say that no other matter has been named; blessed is he who understands it. Seek therein, and be not weary; the result justifies the labour.

A short Appendix and clear Resumption of the foregoing Tract concerning the Great Stone of the Ancient Sages

I, Basil Valentine, brother of the Benedictine Order, do testify that I have written this little book, wherein, after the manner of the Ancients, I have philosophically indicated how this most rare treasure may be acquired, whereby the true Sages did prolong life unto its furthest limit.

But, notwithstanding that my conscience doth bear me witness in the sight of the Most High, before whom all concealed matters are laid bare, that I have written no falsehood, but have so exposed the truth that understanding men can require no further light (that which is laid down in the theoretical part being borne out and confirmed by the practice of the Twelve Keys), yet have I been impelled by various considerations to demonstrate by a shorter way what I have written in the said treatise, and thus cast further light thereon, whereby also the lover of the desired wisdom may obtain an increased illumination for the fulfilment of his desire There are many who will consider that I am speaking too openly, and will hold me answerable for the wickedness that they think will follow, but let them rest assured that it will be sufficiently difficult, notwithstanding, for any thick-headed persons to find what they seek herein. At the same time the matter shall be made clear to the elect. Hearken then, thou follower of truth, to these my words, and so shalt thou find the true way !

Behold, I write nothing more than I am willing to hold by after my death and resurrection! Do thou faithfully and simply lay to heart this shorter way, as hereinafter exhibited, for my words are grounded in simplicity, and my teaching is not confused by a labyrinth of language.

I have already indicated that all things are constituted of three essences - namely, mercury, sulphur, and salt - and herein I have taught what is true. But know that the Stone is composed out of one, two, three, four, and five. Out of five - that is, the quintessence of its own substance. Out of four, by which we must understand the four elements. Out of three, and these are the three principles of all things. Out of two, for the mercurial substance is twofold. Out of one, and this is the first essence of everything which emanated from the primal fiat of creation.

But many may by all these discourses be rendered doubtful in mind as to what they must start with, and as to the consequent theory. So I will, in the first place, speak very briefly concerning Mercury, secondly concerning Sulphur, thirdly concerning Salt; for these are the essence of the Matter of our Stone.

In the first place, you must know that no ordinary quicksilver is useful, but our quicksilver is produced from the best metal by the spagyric art, pure, subtle, clear, and glistening, like a spring, pellucid even as crystal, free from all dross. Hence make water or combustible oil. For Mercury was in the beginning water, and herein all the Sages agree with my dictum and teaching In this oil of Mercury dissolve its own Mercury, from which the water in question was made, and precipitate the Mercury with its own oil. Then we have a twofold mercurial substance; but you must know that gold must first be dissolved in a certain water, as explained in my second Key, after the purification described in the first Key, and must be reduced into a subtle calx, as is mentioned in the fourth Key. Next, this calx must be sublimated by the spirit of salt, again precipitated, and by reverberation reduced into a subtle powder. Then its own sulphur can more easily enter into its substance, and have great friendship with the same, for they have a wondrous love towards each other. Thus you have two substances in one, and it is called Mercury of the Sages, but is yet a single substance, which is the first ferment.

Now follows concerning Sulphur

Seek your Mercury in a similar metal. Then when you know how to extract the metal from its body by purification, the destruction of the first Mars, and reverberation, without the use of any corrosive (the method of doing which I have indicated in my third Key) -- you must dissolve that Mercury in its own blood out of which it was made before it became fixed (as indicated in the sixth Key); and you have then nourished and dissolved the true lion with the blood of the green lion. For the fixed blood of the Red Lion has been made out of the volatile blood of the Green Lion; hence, they are of one nature, and the unfixed blood again renders that which is volatile fixed, and the fixed blood in its turn fixes that which is volatile, as it was before its solution. Then foster it in gentle heat, until the whole of the mercury is dissolved, and you obtain the second ferment (by nourishing the fixed sulphur with that which is not fixed), as all Sages unite with me in testifying. Afterwards this becomes, by sublimation with spirit of wine, of a blood-red colour, and is called potable gold.

Now I will also give my Opinion respecting the Salt of the Sages

The effect of "salt" is to fix or volatilize, according as it is prepared and used. For the spirit of the salt of tartar, if extracted by itself without any addition, has power to render all metals volatile by dissolution and putrefaction, and to dissolve quick or liquid silver into the true mercury, as my practical directions shew.

Salt of tartar by itself is a powerful fixative, particularly if the heat of quicklime be incorporated with it. For these two substances are singularly efficacious in producing fixation.

In the same way, the vegetable salt of wine fixes and volatilizes according to the manner of its preparation. Its use is one of the arcana of Nature, and a miracle of the philosopher's art. When a man drinks wine, there may be gained from his urine a clear salt, which is volatile, and renders other fixed substances volatile, causing them to rise with it in the alembic. But the same does not fix. If a man drank nothing but wine, yet for all that the salt obtained from his urine would have a different property from that gained out of the lees of wine. For it has undergone a chemical change in the human body, having become transmuted from a vegetable into an animal salt -- just as horses that feed on oats, straw, etc., change those vegetable substances into flesh and fat, while the bee prepares honey out of the precious juices of flowers and herbs.

The great change which takes place in these and other substances is due to putrefaction, which separates and transmutes the constituent elements.

The common spirit of salt, which is extracted according to the direction given in my last declaration, if there be added to it a small quantity of the "spirit of the dragon," dissolves, volatilizes, and raises together with itself in the alembic, gold and silver; just as the "eagle," together with the spirit of the dragon (which is found in stony places), before the spirit is separated from its body, is much more powerful in producing fixation than volatility.

This I also say, that if the spirit of common salt be joined to the spirit of wine, and distilled together with it, it becomes sweet, and loses its acidity. This prepared spirit does not dissolve gold bodily, but if it be poured on prepared calx of gold, it extracts the essence of its colour and redness. If this be rightly done, it reduces the white and pure moon to the colour of that body from which it was itself extracted. The old body may also receive back its former colour through the love of alluring Venus, from whose blood it, in the first instance, derived its origin.

But observe, likewise, that the spirit of salt also destroys the moon, and reduces it to a spiritual essence, according to my teaching, out of which the " potable moon " may be prepared. This spirit of the moon belongs to the spirit of the sun, as the female answers to the male, by the copulation or conjunction of the spirit of mercury or its oil.

The spirit lies hid in mercury, the colour you must seek in sulphur, and their coagulation in salt; then you have three things which together are capable of once more generating a perfect thing. The spirit is fermented in the gold with its own proper oil; the sulphur is found in abundance in the property of precious Venus. This kindles the fixed blood which is sprung from it, the spirit of the salt of the Sages imparts strength and firmness, though the spirit of tartar and the spirit of urine together with true vinegar, have great virtue. For the spirit of vinegar is cold, and the spirit of lime is intensely hot, and thus the two spirits are found to be of opposite natures. I do not here speak according to the customary manner of the Sages. But I must not say too openly how the inner gates are to be unlocked.

In bidding farewell, let me impart to you a faithful word. Seek your material in a metallic substance. Thence prepare mercury. This ferment with the mercury of its own proper sulphur, and coagulate them with salt. Distil them together; mix all according to weight. Then you will obtain one thing, consisting of elements sprung from one thing. Coagulate and fix it by means of continuous warmth. Thereupon augment and ferment it a third time, according to the teaching of my two last Keys, and you will find the object and goal of your desire. The uses of the Tincture are set forth plainly in my twelfth Key.

Thanks be to God.

As a parting kindness to you, I am constrained to add that the spirit may also be extracted from black Saturn and benevolent Jupiter. When it has been reduced to a sweet oil, we have a means of robbing the common liquid quicksilver of its vivacity, or rendering it firm and solid, as is also set forth in my book.

Postscript

When you have thus obtained the material, the regimen of the fire is the only thing on which you need bestow much attention. This is the sum and the goal of our search. For our fire is a common fire, and our furnace a common furnace. And though some of my predecessors have left it in writing that our fire is not common fire, I may tell you that it was only one of their devices for hiding the mysteries of our Art. For the material is common, and its treatment consists chiefly in the proper adjustment of the heat to which it is exposed.

The fire of a spirit lamp is useless for our purpose. Nor is there any profit in "horse-dung," nor in the other kinds of heat in the providing of which so much expense is incurred.

Neither do we want many kinds of furnaces. Only our threefold furnace affords facilities for properly regulating the heat of the fire. Therefore do not let any babbling sophist induce you to set up a great variety of expensive furnaces. Our furnace is cheap, our fire is cheap, and our material is cheap - and he who has the material will also find a furnace in which to prepare it, just as he who has flour will not be at a loss for an oven in which it may be baked. It is unnecessary to write a special book concerning this part of the subject. You cannot go wrong, so long as you observe the proper degree of heat, which holds a middle place between hot and cold. If you discover this, you are in possession of the secret, and can practise the Art, for which the CREATOR of all nature be praised world without end. AMEN.